HOURS WITH THE MAS

HEURES AVEC LES MAÎTRES . . . STUNDEN MIT DEN MEISTERN

Pre-1 **Preliminary to Primary**
Vorstufe I

CONTENTS—TABLE DES MATIÈRES—INHALT

Pre-2 **Primary to Elementary**
Vorstufe II

CONTENTS—TABLE DES MATIÈRES—INHALT

Bosworth

Chanson et Danse Bohemienne

Ce morceau est d'humeur enjouée et vive. Jouez-le distinctement, avec des phrases bien définies, les deux accents par mesure doivent être précis, mais nullement martelés. Pour les groupes de deux notes liées des mesures 9 - 11, faites l'exercice indiqué ci-dessous. Jouez la première de chacune des deux notes liées avec une petite insistance (*appuyée*) et la seconde en l'effleurant légèrement du doigt (*atténuée*). Tenez compte des signes concernant la sonorité *en general.*

Bohemian Song and Dance

This piece is cheerful and lively in mood. Play it clearly with well defined phrases, the two accents in a bar to be precise but by no means thumped. For the slurred couplets in bars 9 - 11, practise the exercise given below. Play the first of each two slurred notes with a gentle stress (*weight on*) and the second with light finger touch (*weight off*). Attend to the *general* tone marks.

Böhmisches Tanzlied

Dieses Stück ist heiteren und lebendigen Charakters. Es ist klar und gut phrasiert vorzutragen; die beiden schweren Taktteile müssen rhythmisch genau gespielt, dürfen aber auf keinen Fall überbetont werden. Für das Binden zweier Viertelnoten, wie sie in den Takten 9 - 11 vorkommen, studiere die unten angefügte Übung. Der erste der beiden Töne wird mit etwas Gewicht und der zweite mit zartem, lockerem Anschlag ausgeführt. Beachte die Vortragszeichen.

Exercise on Slurred Couplets
Exercice sur 4 Notes lieés
Übung mit gebunden Viertelnoten

Repeat the first two bars three times, finish with the last two bars
Repetez 3 fois les deux premiéres mesures et finissez en jouant les deux derniéres.
Wiederhole die beiden ersten Takte dreimal und spiele anschliessend die beiden letzen

Made in England
Imprimé en Angleterre

B. & Co. Ltd. 21989

Chanson Heureuse

Ce morceau demande un doigté doux et chantant, les croches de l'accompagnement doivent former un fond moelleux donnant de l'harmonie à ses notes isolées. Avec un seul accent métrique par mesure (sans lourdeur), la musique doit couler en phrases amples, comme l'indiquent les longues liaisons. Là où la mélodie apparait à la main gauche (mesures 5 - 12 et similaires), faites la bien chanter sous l'accompagnement de la main droite.

A Happy Song

This needs a sweet singing touch, the accompanying quavers to make a smooth background which carries harmony in its single notes. With only one metrical accent to-the-bar (not heavy) the music must flow in broad phrases as shown by the long slurs. Where the tune appears in left hand - bars 5-12 and similar - let it sing nicely against right hand part.

Fröhliches Lied

Dieses Lied bedarf einer duftigen, singenden Tongebung; die begleitenden Achtelfiguren müssen einen weichen Untergrund bilden, der mit seinen einzelnen Tönen die Harmonie bestimmt. Die grossen Phrasierungsbögen sind genau zu beachten, und die "eins" erhält jeweils einen zarten Akzent. An den Stellen, wo die linke Hand die Melodieführung übernimmt (wie z.B. in Takt 5 - 12), muss sie sich von der rechten Hand entsprechend abheben.

Le Couppey
1811–1887

Suis mon Conducteur

Il faut une humeur gaie et badine. Jouez avec beacoup de rythme et en accentuant légèrement le "un" de chaque mesure. Indiquez les imitations en faisant ressortir le "conducteur" et en réduisant la sonorité de la partie opposée. Laissez l'imagination seconder l'interprétation.

Follow-My-Leader

A jolly, playful mood is needed. Play very rhythmically with a lightly pointed accent on "one" of each bar. Show the imitations by making the 'leader' stand out and reducing tone in the opposite part. Let imagination help the interpretation.

Spiel zu Zweien

Es gilt, eine lustige, neckische Vortragsweise zu entwickeln. Spiele streng rhythmisch mit leichter Betonung der "eins" eines jeden Taktes. Hebe das jeweils führende Motiv hervor, während die Stimme der anderen Hand etwas zurückgenommen wird. Lasse dich beim Vortrag von deiner eigenen Phantasie leiten.

Un Air de Valse

Ce morceau doit être traité avec grâce. En frappant la noire pointée, et en prenant la croche qui suit sur un ton plus calme, avec un mouvement s'avançant vers la frappe suivante et la mesure suivante, vous pouvez suggérer le tournoiement gracieux et séduisant de la valse. Observez le phrasé moelleux et les inflections au ton ample dans les mesures 5 à 7, 11 et 12, 15 et 16. Gardez constamment le rythme, en tenant compte de l'accentuation seule et unique de la mesure. La main gauche garde la mesure avec ses pulsations *forte*, *faible*, *faible*, mais l'accentuation ne doit, *en aucun cas* être martelée. La pédale contribue à donner de la couleur, si on peut s'en servir facilement.

A Waltz Tune

This piece needs gracious treatment. By stressing the dotted crotchet and taking the ensuing quaver in quieter tone with forward movement to the next beat and next bar, you can suggest the graceful, alluring swing of the waltz. Observe the smooth phrasing and broad tone inflections in bars 5 to 7, 11-12, 15-16. Keep the rhythm steady by attention to the one accent only in a bar. Left hand keeps time with its *strong*, *weak*, *weak* pulses, but *on no account* must the accent be bumped. The pedal helps to add colour, if it can be used easily.

Walzermelodie

Verleihe diesem Stück einen anmutigen Charakter. Durch das Betonen der punktierten Viertelnote und indem man die darauf folgenden Achtelnoten zurückhaltender und zur "eins" des nächsten Taktes hinstrebend spielt, erreicht man den anmutigen bezaubernden Schwung, der dem Walzer zu eigen ist. Achte in den Takten 5-7, 11-12 und 15-16 auf sanfte Phrasierung und geschmeidige Tongebung. Bei gleichbleibendem Rhythmus darf nur die "eins" mit einem Akzent versehen werden. Die linke Hand bestimmt den Rhythmus, wobei das erste Viertel aber auf keinen Fall zu scharf akzentuiert werden darf. Sofern es das Können des Schülers gestattet, wird die Benutzung des Pedals dem Stück noch mehr Farbe verleihen.

Andante

extrait de la Sonatine en Do

Un style de jeu simple, d'un niveau de sonorité généralement léger, l'observance des nuances et un ton doux et chantant dans la mélodie produiront l'effet qui convient. Tenez compte des détails de *staccato*, de *legato* et des petites liaisons, mais surtout rendez le phrasé dans les groupes de quatre mesures, comme l'indiquent les longues liaisons. Etudiez d'abord les accords brisés de la basse comme accords *plaqués*, et ensuite veillez à ce que les croches aient une résonnance bien égale, et forment un fond harmonique pour la mélodie. Faites la plupart des changements de tonalité indiqués.

Andante

from Sonatina in C

A simple style of playing, with generally light tonal level and attention to gradations and a sweet singing tone in the melody, will achieve the right effect. Attend to details of *staccato*, *legato* and small slurs, but overall feel the phrasing in four-bar groups as shown by the long slurs. First study the bass broken chords as *firm* chords, and then see that the quavers sound quite even and form harmonic background for the tune. Make the most of the marked tonal changes.

Andante aus der Sonatine in C-dur

Eine schlichte Spielweise mit im allgemeinen nicht allzu grossem Tonvolumen entspricht der Eigenart dieses Stückes. Hierbei ist auf genaue Dynamik und eine süsse, singende Tongebung in der Melodiestimme zu achten. Berücksichtige das Staccato, Legato und die kleinen Bindebögen, ohne dabei die grossen Phrasierungsbögen ausser Acht zu lassen. Übe den Part der linken Hand zunächst in Akkorden und strebe (im Rhythmus und in der Tongebung) gleichmässige Achtelfiguren als harmonischen Untergrund zur Melodie an. Beachte auf das genaueste alle Vortragsbezeichnungen.

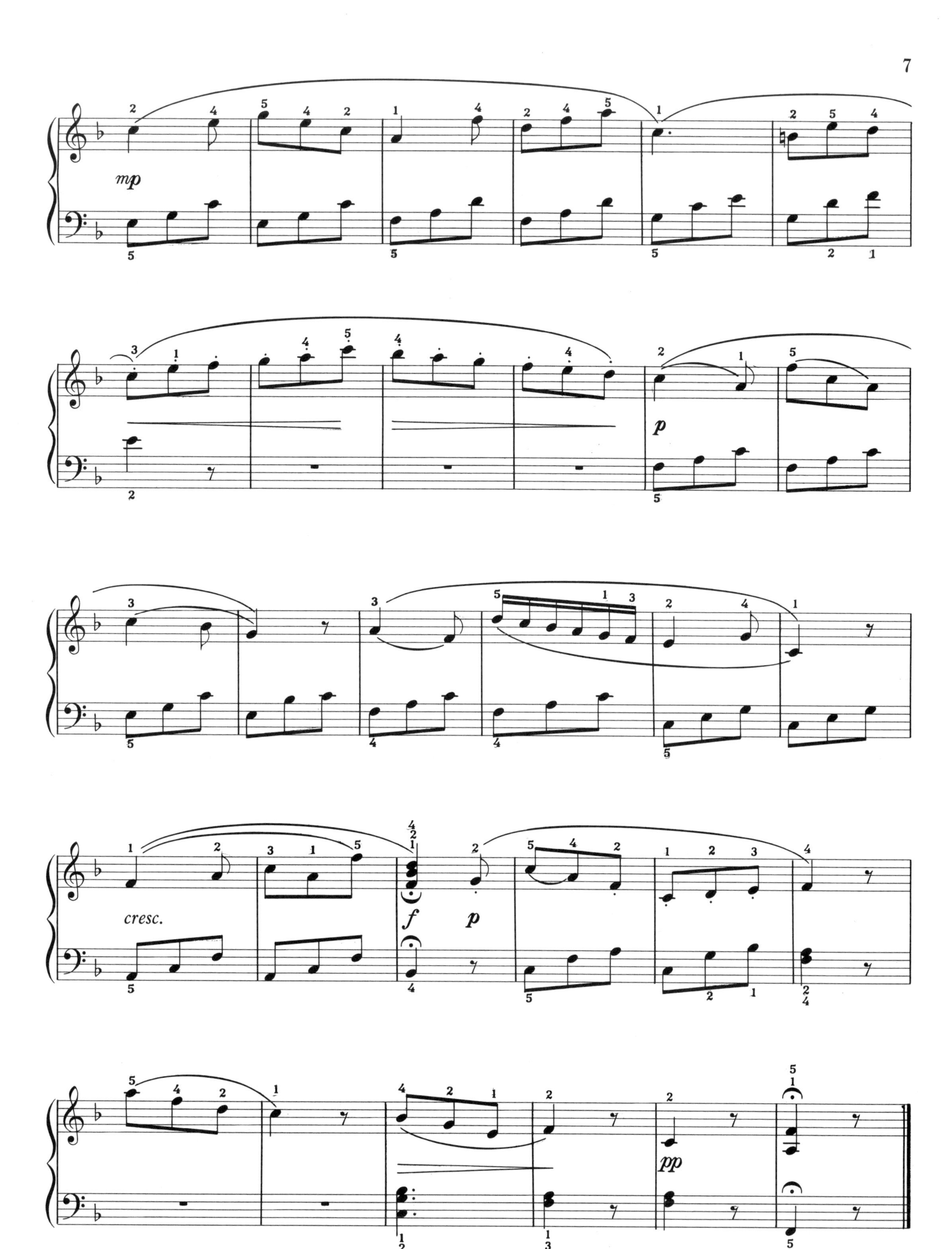
mp
p
cresc.
f
p
pp

Polka

La Polka est une danse bohémienne dont l'origine remonte au début du dix-neuvième siècle, et qui a acquis une popularité formidable dans toute l'Europe. C'est une ronde avec battements fortements marqués et un rythme bondissant. La basse doit être en *staccato* jusqu'au bout, sauf indication différente. Les acciaccaturas aux mesures 4, 8, 12 et 16 doivent être jouées très rapidement sur le battement pour porter l'accent sur la note principale.

Polka

The Polka is a Bohemian dance which originated early in the nineteenth century, and became tremendously popular throughout Europe. It is a round dance with strongly marked beats and a bouncing rhythm. The bass must be *staccato* throughout, except where otherwise marked. Acciaccaturas in bars 4, 8, 12 and 16 must be played very swiftly on the beat to throw an accent on the main note.

Polka

Die Polka ist ein im frühen neunzehnten Jahrhundert in Böhmen entstandener Tanz, der in ganz Europa aussergewöhnlich populär wurde. Sie ist ein Rundtanz mit markantem Taktschlag und strammem Rhythmus. Die Bass-Stimme ist immer, sofern nicht anders notiert, im Staccato zu spielen. Die Vorschläge in den Takten 4, 8, 12 und 16 müssen schnell und auf den Schlag erfolgen, wobei die Hauptnote einen leichten Akzent erhält.

Köhler

Valse

A jouer avec grâce, rythme cadencé et coulant. Les notes sont bien placées sous les doigts et se prêtent à un jeu clair et fluide.

Waltz

To be played gracefully with flowing lilt. The notes lie well under the fingers and invite clear, fluent playing.

Walzer

Dieser Walzer muss graziös und mit überschäumender Freude gespielt werden. Die Töne liegen gut in der Hand und regen zu einer klaren, fliessenden Spielweise an.

Köhler

Hop, Sautez, Dansez

On constatera que les notes sont placées commodément sous les doigts. Quand un changement de position se produit, comme à la fin des mesures 4, 5, 6 et endroits similaires, il n'y a qu'à mouvoir nettement l' avant-bras pour que les doigts se trouvent au-dessus de leurs nouvelles touches. Le rythme des croches et doubles croches pointées est désigné par les noms de durée en Français: ta - è - fè, ta - è - fè etc. ou simplement par les mots: *Hop sautez et hop sautez et hop sautez dansez*. Les notes de la main droite à partir de la fin de la mesure 14 courent doucement en une légère "ruade" de *staccato*. Les doubles croches doivent être plus calmes que les notes pointées.

Hop, Skip and Jump

It will be found that the notes lie easily under the fingers. When a change of position occurs, as at the end of bars 4, 5, 6 and similar places, just move the forearm neatly to bring the fingers over their new keys. The dotted-quaver-semiquaver rhythm is helped by the use of French time-names: *ta-e-fe, ta-e-fe* etc. or simply the words: *Hop and Skip and hop and skip and hop and skip and jump*. The R.H. notes from the end of bar 14 run smoothly into a light 'kick-off' *staccato*. Semiquavers must be quieter than dotted note.

Eins, zwei, drei

Dieses Stück liegt gut in der Hand. Im Falle einer Veränderung der Lage der Hand, wie z.B. in den Takten 4, 5 und 6, bedarf es nur einer eleganten Bewegung des Unterarms, um die Hand über den neu zu spielenden Tönen in Stellung zu bringen. Der Rhythmus der punktierten Achtel mit einem Sechzehntel lässt sich unter Zuhilfenahme der Wortfolge: eins und zwei und drei und vier usw. leicht einprägen. Die am Ende von Takt 14 einsetzenden Sechzehntelnoten laufen sanft hinunter in das angehängte staccatierte Achtel. Die den punktierten Achteln folgenden Sechzehntelnoten sollen etwas zarter gespielt werden als die punktierten Noten.

Czerny

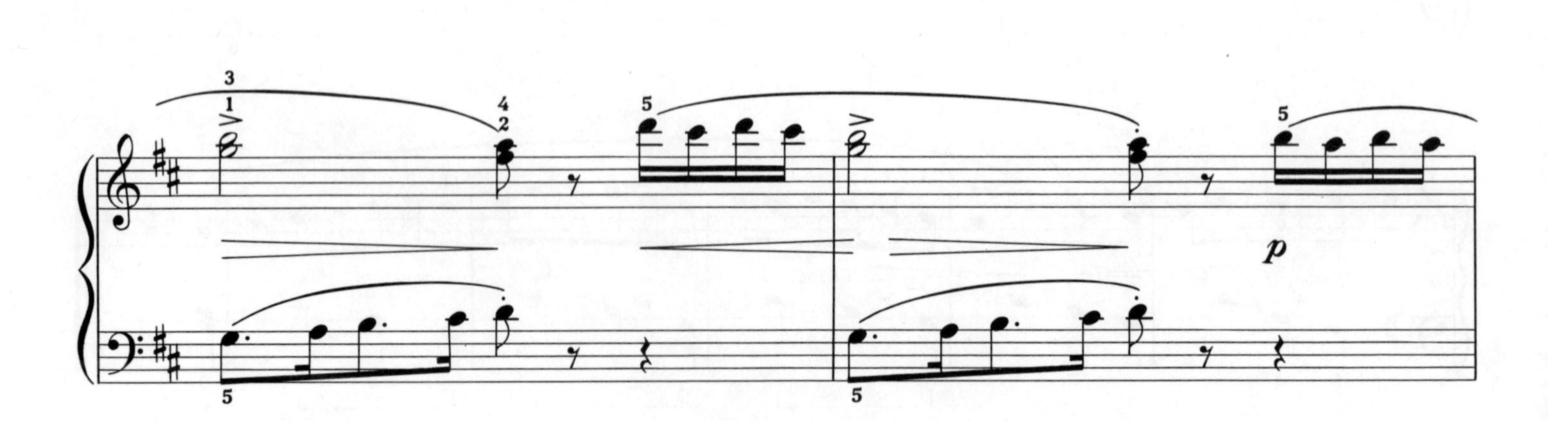

f
p
f

La marche militaire
Op. 68, no. 2

Le rythme doit être très décidé avec articulation claire et frappe tranchante et animée. Assurez-vous qu'aux deux mains les notes résonnent ensemble avec précision. Observez la graduation de sonorité et donnez aux notes de *tenuto* (—) leur pleine valeur - en ne faisant que les détacher. Posez bien les mains au-dessus des touches et maintenez ferme le bout des doigts, afin de faire ressortir la mélodie qui se trouve au sommet des intervalles et des accords.

Soldiers' March
Op. 68, No. 2

The rhythm must be very decided with clear articulation and crisp, lively touch. Ensure that the notes in both hands sound precisely together. Attend to tone gradations, and give the *tenuto* (—) notes their full value—only just detached. Shape the hands well over the keys and keep the finger tips firm, in order to bring out the melody lying at the top of intervals and chords.

Soldatenmarsch

Ein präziser Rhythmus mit klarer Artikulation und ein frischer, lebendiger Anschlag sind in diesem Stück notwendig. Die Noten beider Hände müssen ganz genau gleichzeitig erklingen. Beachte die Dynamik und spiele die mit einem "tenuto" versehenen Töne voll aus (bei nur geringem Sichabheben der Töne voneinander). Bringe die Hand in genaue Stellung über die zu spielenden Töne und nehme mit den Fingerspitzen eine feste Haltung ein, um die über den Akkorden liegende Melodie deutlich hörbar herausarbeiten zu können.

Schumann
1810–1856

Un Air de Chanson

Une bonne sonorité chantante et un phrasé moelleux sont nécessaires. Omettez tous les enjolivements, jusqu'à ce que vous connaissiez bien l'air, et puis adaptez les bien, de façon à ne pas déranger le rythme.

A Song Tune

Good singing tone and smooth phrasing are needed. Omit all the ornaments until the tune is well known, and then fit them in neatly, so as not to disturb the rhythm.

Melodie

Benötigt werden hier ein singender Ton und geschmeidige Phrasierung. Lasse zunächst die Verzierungen beim Üben weg, bis du die Melodie genau (rhythmisch) kennst, und füge sie dann so geschickt ein, dass der rhythmische Ablauf nicht gestört wird.

Purcell
1659—1695

Cantabile ♩ = 100

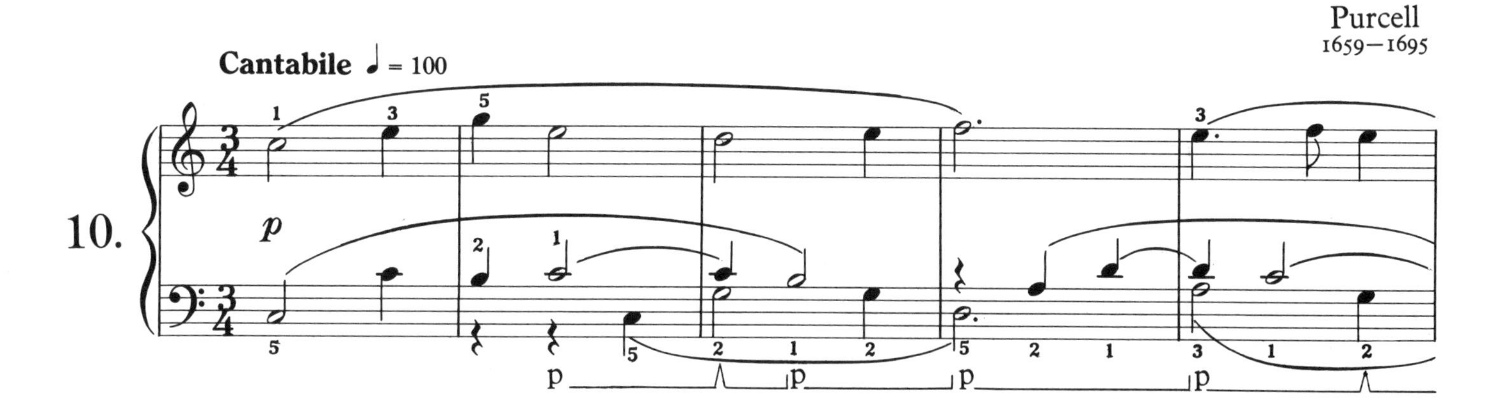

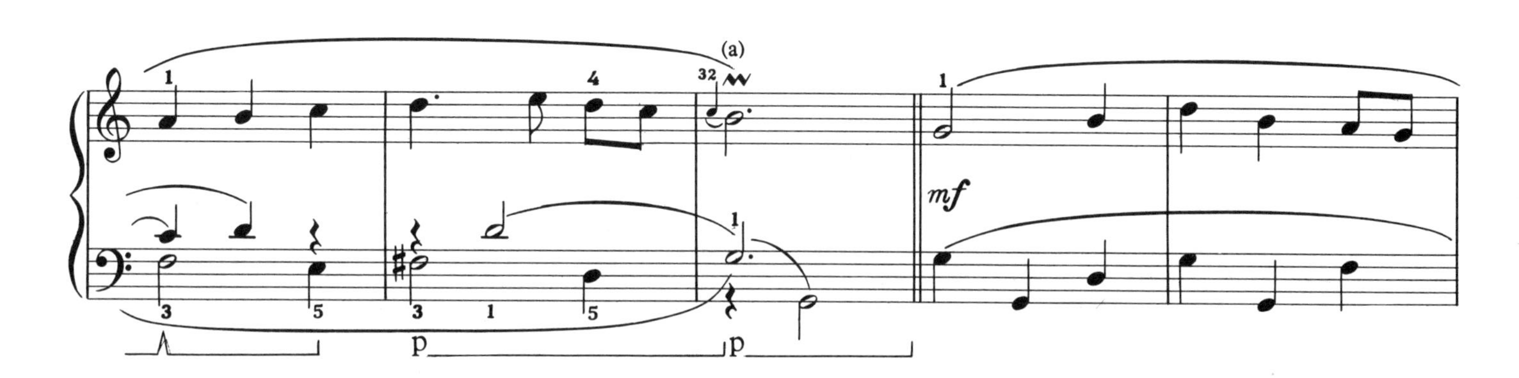

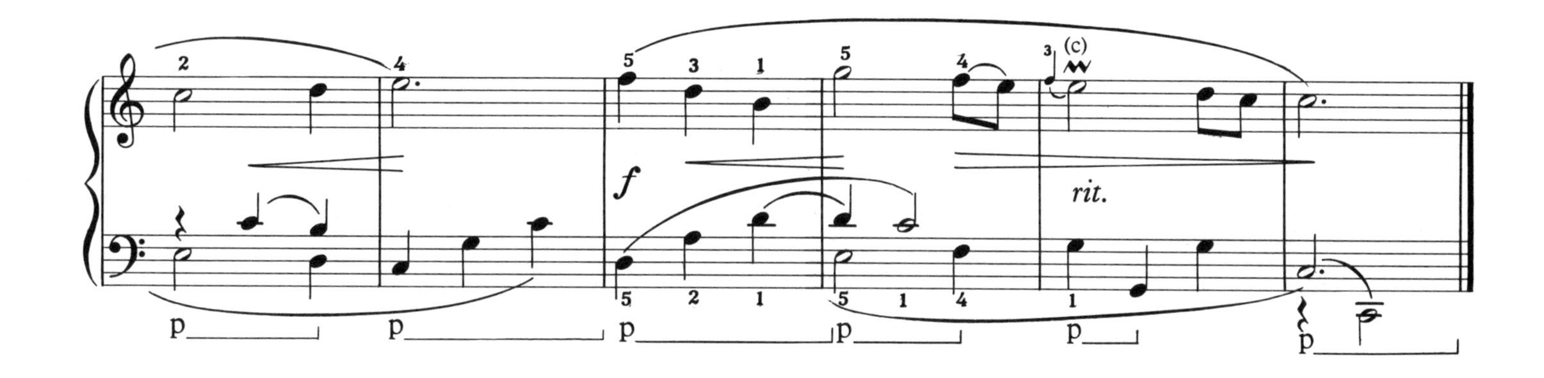

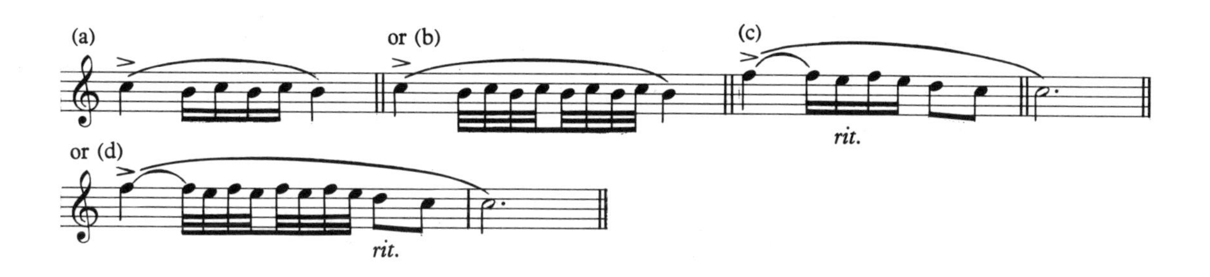

Haut vol

Les graduations de sonorité sont importantes pour donner une sensation d'espace et de liberté de mouvement. Conservez le moelleux de la basse et laissez les accents sur les valeurs des première et quatrième croches (sans lourdeur, s'il vous plait), conservez les pulsations du rythme.

Flying High

Tone gradations are important to give a sense of space and freedom of movement. Keep the bass smooth and let the accents on first and fourth quaver values (not heavy, please) keep the rhythm pulsing.

Höhenflug

Eine genaue Dynamik ist insofern wichtig, als es die Vorstellung eines weiten Raumes und ungehemmter Bewegungsfreiheit zu vermitteln gilt. Bei pulsierendem Rhythmus und weich zu spielendem Bass sind das erste und vierte Achtel jedes Taktes *leicht* zu betonen.

Czerny
1791–1857

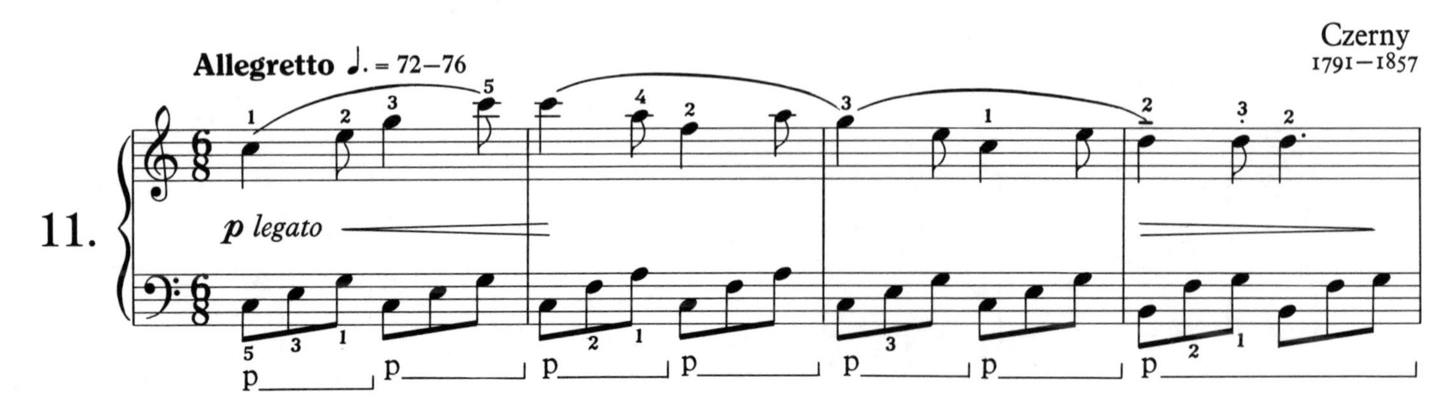

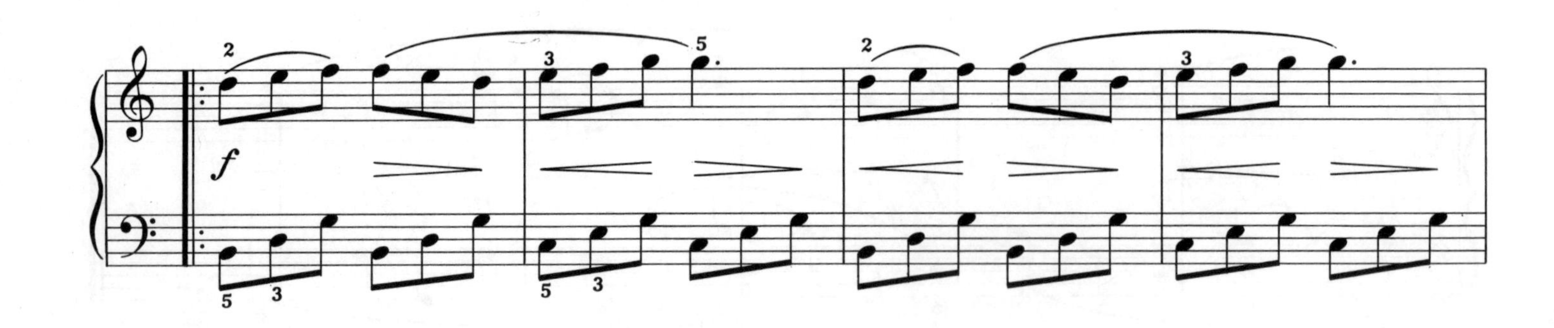

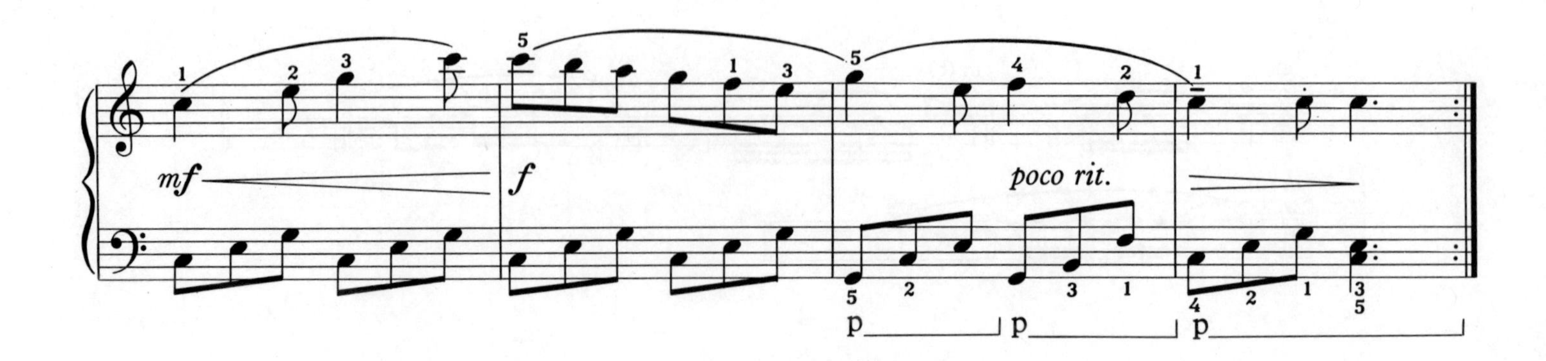

Andante

Il faut ici un rythme doux et cadencé, avec un accent seulement par mesure. Pour éviter l'effet d'un triolet dans la mesure 10, donnez à la note du milieu d'un groupe de trois un peu plus d'importance qu'aux autres. Observez les nuances des terminaisons *feminines*—mesures 8 et 16.

Andante

A gentle lilting rhythm is needed here, with one accent only to a bar. To avoid the effect of a triplet in bar 10, make the middle note of a group of three slightly more important than the others. Attend to tone shading at *feminine* endings - bars 8 and 16.

Andante

Dieses Stück erfordert einen sanften, wiegenden Rhythmus mit nur einem Akzent pro Takt. Um in Takt 10 die drei Achtelnoten nicht als Triole erscheinen zu lassen, erhält die mittlere Note etwas mehr Gewicht als die anderen. Achte in den Takten 8 und 16 auf das "decrescendo", um eine tonlich weiche Schlussbildung zu erzielen.

A. E. Müller
1767—1817

Calme du Soir

Abaissez doucement les touches et faites chanter la mélodie au sommet des intervalles et des accords.

Evening Calm

Weigh the keys down gently and let the melody sing at the top of intervals and chords.

Abendstille

Spiele mit zartem Anschlag und lasse die über den Intervallen und Akkorden liegende Melodie klar hervortreten.

Czerny

Menuet en Fa

Ceci est un spécimen notoire de menuet. Imaginez-le joué par un trio d'instruments à cordes avec des valeurs de temps et une sonorité soigneusement équilibrées.

Minuet in F

This is a stately type of minuet. Imagine it as played by a trio of stringed instruments, with time and tone values carefully balanced.

Menuett

Dieses Menuett hat einen feierlichen Charakter. Stelle es dir von einem Streichtrio gespielt vor und achte genau auf die Notenwerte und das Tempo.

Une Danse Gracieuse

Les petites liaisons signifient *legato* et ne troublent pas l'accentuation normale. Faites des mouvements faciles partant du poignet, et faites en sorte que les doigts soient toujours prêts au-dessus de leurs touches. Les longues liaisons indiquent le phrasé.

A Graceful Dance

The small slurs are for *legato* and do not disturb the normal accentuation. Make easy movements from the wrist and have the fingers neatly prepared over their keys. Long slurs show the phrasing.

Grazioser Tanz

Die kleinen Bindebögen bezeichnen das Legatospiel, während die normale Akzentuierung dadurch nicht beeinträchtigt wird. Spiele leicht aus dem Handgelenk und halte die Finger genau über den anzuschlagenden Tasten in Bereitschaft. Die grossen Bögen zeigen die Phrasierung an.

Le Couppey
1811–1887

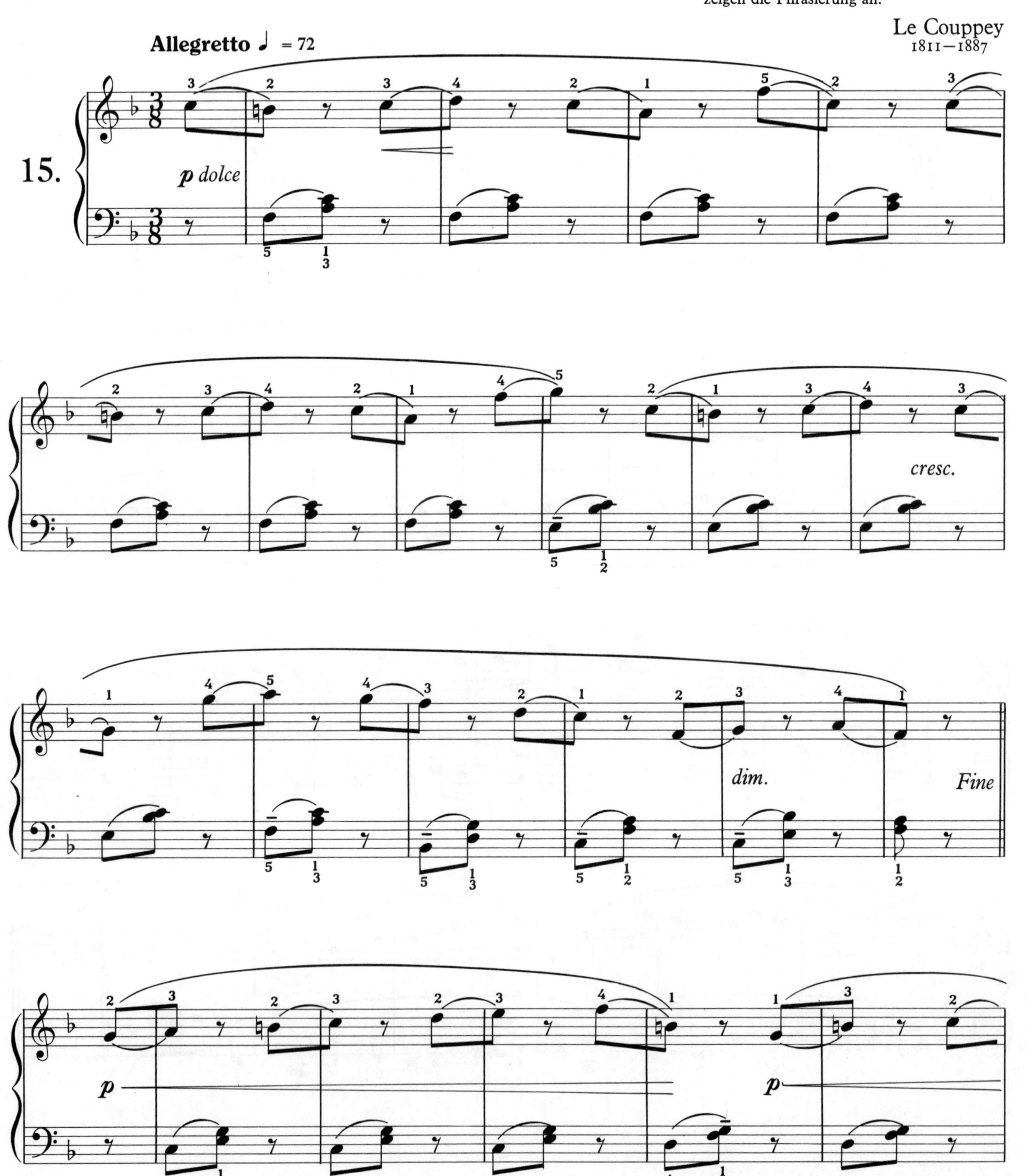

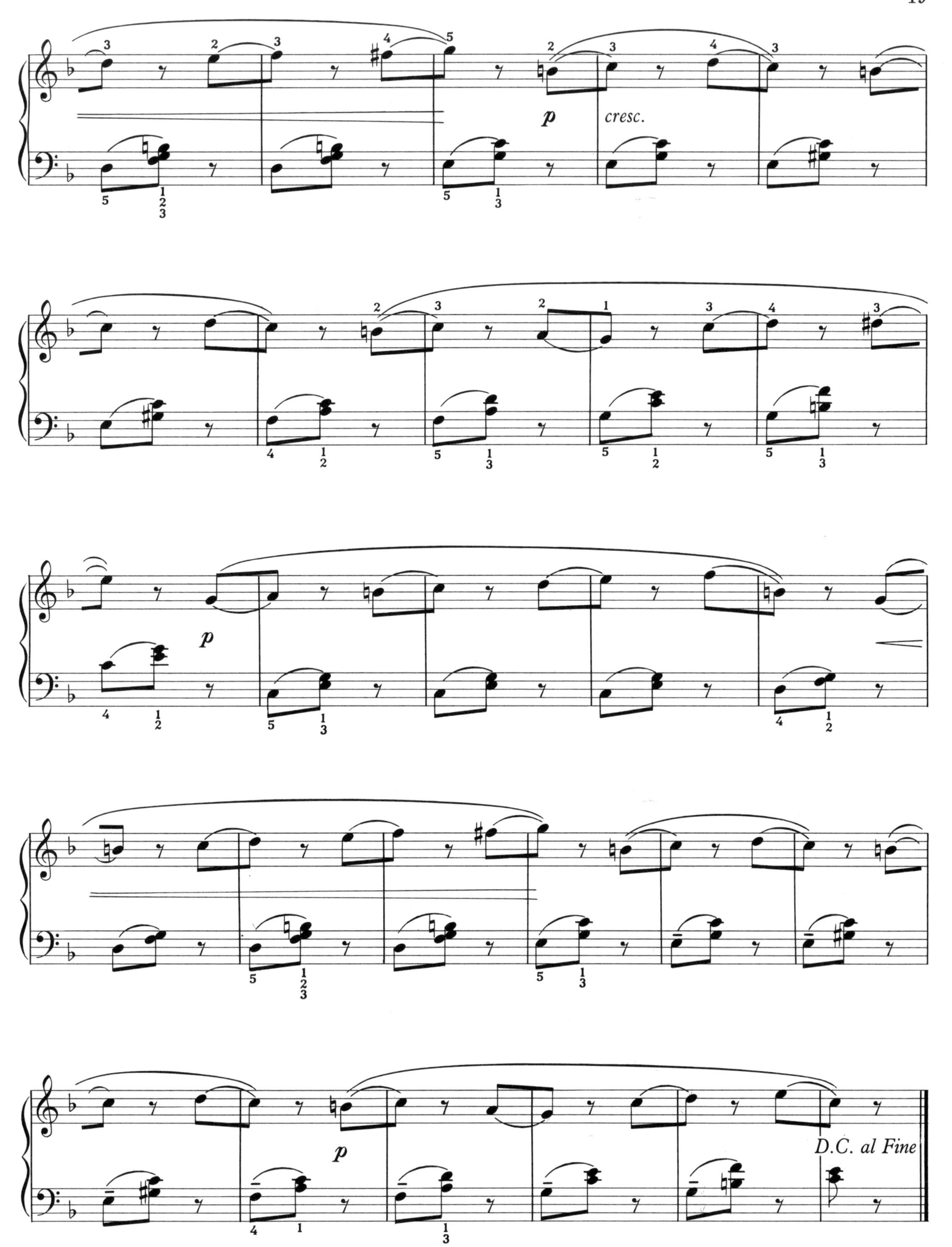
p
cresc.
p
p
D.C. al Fine

Une Danse Campagnarde

Ce morceau serait à jouer avec un sentiment d'amusement, une bonne progression rythmique et une accentuation claire. Le jeu des triolets doit être moelleux - pas de rupture entre les groupes. En plus de l'accent normal sur le "un" et le "trois" des quatre temps, il faudrait un accent légèrement pointé sur la première note de chaque triolet afin que l'auditeur perçoive une ligne claire et mélodique, comme l'indique la note du bas (a).

A Country Dance

This should be played with a sense of enjoyment, good rhythmic progression and clear accentuation. The triplets must be played smoothly - no break between the groups. In addition to the normal accent on "one" and "three" of 4/4 time, there should be a lightly pointed accent on the first of each triplet, so that the listener is conscious of a clear melodic line, as shown in footnote (a).

Bauerntanz

Eine ausgelassene Grundstimmung, treibender Rhythmus und klare Akzentuierung sind hier anzustreben. Die Triolen müssen fliessend und ohne Unterbrechung zwischen den einzelnen Gruppen gespielt werden. Neben der üblichen Betonung der "eins" und der "drei" im 4/4-Takt sollte auch die erste Note jeder Triolengruppe einen leichten Akzent erhalten, damit dem Zuhörer die klare melodische Linie, wie sie in der Fussnote angezeigt ist, bewusst wird.

Berceuse

Les mesures d'introduction et les notes de basse devraient presque partout résonner comme des cordes doucement princées pour former un fond de mélodie moelleux. Faites en sorte que la double croche qui suit une croche pointée ait une sonorité beaucoup plus calme que la note plus longue, et veillez à l'exactitude de sa durée pour produire un agréable effet de balancement.

Lullaby

The introductory bars and the bass notes almost throughout should sound like gently plucked strings to form a background of the soothing melody. Make the semiquaver which follows a dotted quaver much quieter in tone than the longer note, and see to its exact timing to achieve a gentle rocking effect.

Wiegenlied

Die Einleitungstakte und, fast während des ganzen Stückes, die Bass-Stimme sollen als Untergrund zur ruhigen Melodiestimme wie das zarte Zupfen auf Streichinstrumenten klingen. Die der punktierten Achtelnote folgende Sechzehntelnote muss sehr viel leiser als diese angeschlagen werden. Halte den Rhythmus genau ein, um den Eindruck des leichten Hinundherwiegens zu erzeugen.

Kullak
1818–1882

a tempo
rall.
p
a tempo
rall.
p
mf

Processed and printed by
Halstan & Co. Ltd., Amersham, Bucks., England

HOURS WITH THE MASTERS

By DOROTHY BRADLEY

CONTENTS

VOLUME 1. Primary and Elementary

1.	**Mozart**	Minuet in F, No. 1
2.	**Mozart**	Minuet in F, K.5
3.	**Schumann**	Melody, Op. 68, No, 1
4.	**Schumann**	Humming Song, Op. 68, No. 3
5.	**Schumann**	A Little Study, Op, 68, No. 14
6.	**Bach**	Minuet in G (from Anna Magdalena Book)
7.	**Bach**	Minuet in A minor (from Anna Magdalena Book)
8.	**Diabelli**	Rondo in C, No. 12 ("First Piano Lessons")
9.	**Diabelli**	Allegretto in C, No. 10 ("First Piano Lessons")
10.	**Bertini**	Rondo No. 3, from "Petits Morceaux"
11.	**Purcell**	Minuet in G
12.	**Pleyel**	Rondo Militaire
13.	**Clementi**	Sonatina in C, Op. 36, No. 1 (last movement)
14.	**Haydn**	Allegro in F
15.	**Bach**	March in D
16.	**Purcell**	March in C
17.	**Steibelt**	Ländler in A
18.	**Beethoven**	Rondo from Sonatina in F
19.	**Beethoven**	Ecossaise in G
20.	**Couperin**	Le Petit Rien
21.	**Clementi**	Andante from Sonatina in F, Op. 36, No. 4
22.	**Clementi**	Sonatina in C, Op. 36, No. 3 (first movement)
23.	**Kuhlau**	Allegro Vivace from Sonatina in C
24.	**Schumann**	Siciliano, Op. 68, No. 11
25.	**Heller**	Berceuse (Study in C) Op. 47, No. 19
26.	**Burgmuller**	L'Harmonie des Anges, Op. 100, No. 21
27.	**Gurlitt**	Slumber Song, Op. 224, No. 1

VOLUME 2. Transitional

1.	**Haydn**	Minuet and Trio (from Small Sonata in D)
2.	**J. S. Bach**	Prelude in C minor
3.	**Schumann**	Hunting Song, Op. 68, No. 7
4.	**Schumann**	Song of the Reapers, Op. 68, No. 18
5.	**Gurlitt**	Minuet, op. 224, No. 4
6.	**A. E. Müller**	Scherzo
7.	**Handel**	Prelude in G, (from Seven Pieces)
8.	**Mozart**	Minuet and Trio, from Sonatina in C
9.	**C. P. E. Bach**	Allegretto (from Sonata in F)
10.	**Purcell**	Gavotte
11.	**Bertini**	Andante in A, (Petits Morceaux, No. 11)
12.	**Bertini**	Scherzo (Petits Morceaux, No. 12.)
13.	**Schumann**	The Poor Orphan, Op. 68, No. 6
14.	**J. Ph. Rameau**	Rigaudon
15.	**Handel**	Courante in F
16.	**Gurlitt**	Impromptu, Op. 224, No. 5
17.	**Beethoven**	Bagatelle, Op. 33, No. 3
18.	**Beethoven**	Scherzando from Sonata in D
19.	**Schumann**	Doll's Cradle Song, Op, 118, No.1.
20.	**Bach J. S.**	Courante, from Wilhelm Friedemann Bach Book
21.	**Mozart**	Rondo from Sonata in C, K.545
22.	**Jensen**	The Mill, Op. 17, No. 3

VOLUME 3. Lower

1.	**Arne**	Jig in C, from Sonata No. 6.
2.	**Dussek**	Minuetto.
3.	**Frescobaldi**	Corrente.
4.	**Clementi**	Sonatina in D. First Movement, Op. 36, No. 6.
5.	**Bach**	Minuet No.1, from French Suite in B Minor, No.3.
6.	**Brahms**	Waltz in D Minor, Op. 39, No. 5.
7.	**Beethoven**	Bagatelle in D, Op. 33, No. 6.
8.	**Schubert**	Ecossaise in B Minor.
9.	**Heller**	Etude in E Minor (Tarantelle) Op. 46, No. 7.
10.	**Handel**	Gigue from Suite No. 16.
11.	**Bach**	Gavotte.
12.	**Byrd**	Pavane. "The Earle of Salisbury".
13.	**Bach**	Prelude in F.
14.	**Bach**	Bourrée.
15.	**Schumann**	Rustic Song, Op. 68, No. 20.
16.	**Rameau**	Gigue en Rondeau.
17.	**Haydn**	Minuet from Sonata in D.
18.	**Couperin**	Le Moucheron.
19.	**Schumann**	Waltz. Op. 124, No. 4.
20.	**Heller**	Etude in C, Op. 45. No. 1.
21.	**Beethoven**	Für Elise.
22.	**Gade**	Elegy, Op. 19, No. 1.
23.	**Mozart**	Allegro from Sonata in C. K. 545.
24.	**Mendelssohn**	Song Without Words, Op. 30, No. 3.

VOLUME 4. Higher

1.	**Arne**	Minuet with Variations
2.	**Bach**	Gavotte in G, from French Suite No. 5.
3.	**Bach**	Gigue in B minor, from French Suite No. 3.
4.	**Rameau**	La Joyeuse. (Rondeau)
5.	**Beethoven**	First Movement from Sonatina in C
6.	**Mendelssohn**	Song Without Words, Op. 19, No. 2.
7.	**Bach**	Polonaise in E, from French Suite No. 6.
8.	**Beethoven**	Bagatelle, Op. 119, No. 1.
9.	**Couperin**	Les Petites Moulins à Vent
10.	**Bach**	Two-part Invention No. 4., in D minor
11.	**Haydn**	Gipsy Rondo, From Trio in C
12.	**Beethoven**	Bagatelle, Op. 119, No. 4.
13.	**Purcell**	Prelude in C, from 5th Suite
14.	**Jensen**	Lied, Op. 33, No. 10.
15.	**Mozart**	Two Minuets from Sonata in E flat
16.	**Haydn**	Finale from Sonata in D
17.	**Chopin**	Mazurka in C, Op, 33.
18.	**Schumann**	Bunte Blätter No. 1, Op. 99.
19.	**Jensen**	Longing, Op. 8, No. 5.
20.	**Kerjulf**	Spring Song, Op. 28, No. 5.
21.	**Handel**	Gigue from Suite in D minor

VOLUME 5. Intermediate

1.	**Handel**	Allemande from Suite No. 16.
2.	**Arne**	First Movement from Sonata in A
3.	**Bach**	Sarabande from French Suite No. 1.
4.	**Bach**	Air and Allemande from Suite No. 4.
5.	**Chopin**	Prelude in E minor No. 4.
6.	**Ph. E. Bach**	Solfeggietto
7.	**Schumann**	Albumleaf in E flat Op. 99.
8.	**Daquin**	Le Coucou
9.	**Couperin**	Le Commere
10.	**Schumann**	May, Charming May, Op. 68, No. 13.
11.	**Handel**	Fantasia in C
12.	**Beethoven**	Andante from Sonata, Op. 14, No. 2.
13.	**Schumann**	Fantasie-Dance, Op. 124.
14.	**Schumann**	Catch Me If You Can, Op. 15, No. 3.
15.	**Bach**	Three-Part Invention, No. 11.
16.	**Brahms**	Waltz in B minor, Op. 39, No. 11.
17.	**Mendelssohn**	Song Without Words, Op. 85, No. 1.
18.	**Beethoven**	Rondo in A
19.	**Mozart**	Allegro from Sonatina in A
20.	**Schubert**	Moment Musical, Op, 49, No. 3.
21.	**Heller**	Arabesque, Op. 49, No. 1.
22.	**Chopin**	Mazurka in B flat Op. 7, No. 1.

VOLUME 6. Advanced

1.	**Franz Liszt**	Consolation No. 5
2.	**Couperin**	Le Bavolet Flottant
3.	**Bach**	Three-Part Invention, No. 13
4.	**Rameau**	Le Rappel Des Oiseaux
5.	**Mendelssohn**	No. 2 of Two Musical Sketches
6.	**Schumann**	Warum?
7.	**Brahms**	Waltz in A flat, Op. 39, No. 15
8.	**J. Field**	Nocturne in B flat, No. 5
9.	**Schubert**	Musical Moment, Op. 94, No. 5
10.	**Chopin**	Prelude, Op. 28, No. 3
11.	**Schumann**	Novelette in D, Op. 21, No. 4
12.	**Chopin**	Mazurka in C minor, Op. 30, No. 1
13.	**Stephen Heller**	Tarantelle in A flat, Op. 85, No. 2

BOSWORTH & CO. LTD.